Communication

Conversational Abilities And Communication Methods
Regarding Living With Difficult Individuals

*(The Ultimate Guide To Improving Your Conversational
Skills And Overcoming Shyness)*

Brendan Armitage

TABLE OF CONTENT

Introduction 1

Chapter 1: Methods To A Resolution 10

Chapter 2: When Is Criticism Unacceptable? 17

Chapter 3: The Hidden Obstacles To Effective Communication And How To Overcome Them 33

Chapter 4: What Hinders Your Ability To Communicate Effectively? 42

Chapter 5: Body Language 53

Chapter 6: A Knowledge Of Body Language 58

Chapter 7: How To Improve Your Physical Presentation 63

Chapter 8: Developing Expertise In Non-Verbal Communication 68

Chapter 9: Genuinely Smile To Make Others Feel Distinguished. 75

Chapter 10: Who Are Intelligent Negotiators? 85

Chapter 11: The Ritualistic Nature Of Negotiating 94

Chapter 12: Manage And Pro-Actively 108

Chapter 13: Conflict Management And Difficult Dialogue 116

Chapter 14: Identifying And Resolving Conflict Origins 124

Chapter 15: Setting Boundaries And Establishing Rules 128

Chapter 16: Expressly And Seriously 133

Chapter 17: Resolve The Underlying Tensions In Your Relationships. 145

Conclusion.. 161

Introduction

If a leader is to remain a leader, he or she must possess exceptional interpersonal skills. A leader is a person who plays a prominent role in a business or division within that business. In addition, there are strict, political, and local leaders, chiefs of organizations and groups, etc. In this guide, we will examine business leaders and how relational skills are an essential component of effective administration.

We should commence with a definition of a good leader and how their correspondence style and decisions demonstrate that they are a good leader.

What You Say and Don't Say Is Significant

However, if the worker believes that they are being laid off because you "could do without them" or because of some form of discrimination, a detailed description of the situation could create a minefield of legal liability. Allegations of racism, sexism, ageism, and other forms of discrimination can impair your organization and expose it to severe financial consequences.

Therefore, it is essential that you, as the leader, establish a clear protocol for addressing all specialists, which you will then communicate to all supervisors and employees. Any crude remarks, harassing, or aggressive tendencies should be discouraged consistently and across all platforms, including email and web-based entertainment accounts, as well as face-to-face interactions between partners. Indeed, "harmless prodding" can be detrimental and appear harassing to some individuals.

Continuing on

Whenever something substantial is communicated, follow-up can have a significant impact on the difference between success and failure.

Using the above model for layoffs, it will be essential to conduct one more meeting to discuss the subsequent stages with the remaining employees. In addition, it will be necessary to hold meetings in order to ensure that each task performed by those who have been laid off will be completed.

Being Observable

When difficulties become overwhelming, even the most capable leaders must retreat to their office and hide. Nonetheless, being conspicuous is frequently one of the most remarkable forms of administration. Similarly, an entryway strategy in which individuals feel they can approach you with various types of feedback and that these will be taken seriously and treated with deference can be effective.

Developing the Mood

Often, the most important aspect of authority is establishing the atmosphere. A positive, playful leader with a lethal instinct is more likely to gain followers than someone who consistently conveys regrettable messages. In any case, a leader with strong relational skills will want to reevaluate the situation in order to maintain a devoted following when circumstances are dire.

For example, regarding layoffs, it should be clarified that these temporary losses are being made for long-term gains.

In the event that two divisions are merged, a good leader would demonstrate the overall benefits and how the task can be accomplished more efficiently.

Transmitting Change

Many people cannot tolerate change. In spite of the fact that it is an unavoidable reality, people have become so accustomed to their routines that any change can be extremely upsetting and even appear to be a threat to all existence. Having compassion for this perspective can aid in streamlining the changes, despite the fact that it is not usually legitimate.

Organizing Regular Gatherings

Customary gatherings provide an opportunity to communicate clearly and solicit input. Try not to hold gatherings for the sake of holding them. Have distinct meeting objectives, plans, and activity projects at the conclusion of each gathering. Follow up promptly on any activity steps that result from these meetings.

Being a Good Listener

Many individuals believe that speaking effectively is essential to being an effective leader. A truly competent pioneer also listens. They are compassionate, value others' opinions, and are perpetually learning from others, as opposed to believing they have all the answers.

Recognize that people are merely human. Everyone has shortcomings. In the event that an error was made, determine the reasons why it was successful. Listen in and express your thoughts.

Consider ideas and developments. If you believe that the individual deserves a second chance, give them one.

Treat coworkers as you would want your finest supervisor to treat you. We will never be able to see the world from another person's perspective, but we can try to be understanding and forgiving when they are experiencing professional or personal difficulties, so that everyone feels valued.

Never Allow

Always be precise in your verbal and written communications. After a telephone conversation or group meeting, confirm any pertinent information that has been recorded on paper, including email. Check and double-check, especially when any deadlines are approaching. In your correspondences, for instance, it is more prudent to briefly summarize key points and dates and repeat the same information than to assume that everybody is aware of the information when they may not be.

If you are a business leader, these are likely the most important aspects of effective correspondence. Your approach will vary considerably depending on whether the communication is verbal or written. We should seek for verbal communication in the subsequent segment.

Compelling VERBAL Correspondence

Verbal correspondence is frequently undervalued due to the fact that we can all communicate verbally, regardless of our journalistic abilities. However, effective verbal communication does not come naturally to everyone. Fortunately, a skill can be mastered with some time and effort.

Chapter 1: Methods To A Resolution

Entering into a conflict situation is the simplest aspect of life, as it is frequently inadvertent. Extricating yourself from a tense situation, however, requires a great deal more delicacy and grace, as well as an array of skills to ensure that the situation does not escalate.

Reacting to Criticism Made of You

Even if there are no flaws, someone will always find something to criticize, regardless of how hard you strive to please everyone all the time. Depending on the volatility of your temper, you will either disregard it as a minor annoyance or respond in kind.

Criticism Described

We are acquainted with two varieties of criticism. The first is constructive, while the second is negative.

Positive and negative feedback are permitted by constructive criticism, but both are designed and delivered in a way that promotes development and enhanced performance. This can be provided by a loved one or a supervisor regarding a particular endeavor.

Negative criticism inhibits growth and is frequently perceived as insulting and degrading, undermining the time and effort invested in a project.

Criticism is an essential component of the work performed, particularly when a team has become unproductive or complacent. It is inevitable that you will receive criticism, some of which will be fair and some not, and there are methods to deal with it.

Controlling your reaction—your work ethic will be determined by your response to criticism, and specifically by your level of professionalism; this includes your body language more than your words. To avoid a reflexive response, take a long breath and count to five while maintaining facial control.

Don't take it personally; because we devote so much of ourselves to our work, we frequently take criticism personally. When you are able to separate yourself from your work, you will realize that your professional errors do not define you as a person.

If you internalize criticism and fail to analyze what it means objectively, you will become defensive and make excuses instead of using the feedback to better yourself. When you implement these changes, you demonstrate your maturity and capacity for self-reflection.

Recognize your humanity; making mistakes is part of being human, and everyone, whether novice or expert, will fail. It is essential to acknowledge that it occurred and, as stated previously, to find a method to take corrective action.

Be appreciative; it's not always simple to sincerely thank someone for their feedback, particularly if it's sincere and intended to help you rather than to tear you down. It was likely just as uncomfortable for them as it was for you.

Be contrite. When you pause before responding to criticism, you are able to analyze the feedback and acknowledge the possibility that their words contain some truth. Even if your ego has been wounded, you can only benefit from the experience.

Give a straightforward apology; simply apologize with no explanations unless the conversation calls for them. A profuse contrition could appear insincere and make the conversation uncomfortable.

You have a tendency to ruminate on things you perceive as negative, and you tend to internalize the negative instead of focusing on the positive; this prevents you from altering your behavior to improve your performance.

Changing Your Attitude Toward Criticism

When receiving feedback, focus on what is true and disregard what does not apply to you personally, particularly if the feedback pertains to a team project. Utilize the negative aspects of the feedback in order to improve your performance. There are multiple methods to find the positive in any given feedback:

Who is the critic? In the vast majority of cases, your colleagues want the best results for your work and want to help you improve. This will help you identify areas for improvement.

Self-awareness is essential—acknowledge that the criticism hurt and investigate the reasons why so that you can heal, particularly if it is related to your past.

Listen to what is being said; rather than hearing the words to defend yourself, listen so that you can interpret the meaning of the words and use them to your advantage.

Respect the criticism; negative criticism can be just as valuable as positive criticism and can have a greater impact on your work ethic because it effects a change opportunity.

Use the feedback as a learning opportunity and, as difficult as it may be, try not to let it influence your confidence. Utilize this opportunity to observe how criticism effects you and how it can assist you in the future when you must provide feedback.

Commentary on the Workplace

Your team requires feedback to ensure they are on the correct path. This enables the team to make the necessary modifications to a project to ensure everyone's satisfaction. When they do not receive any feedback, whether constructive or not, they will either assume the endeavor is perfect and continue as they were, or they will determine that it is not worth their time or effort to provide feedback.

Chapter 2: When Is Criticism Unacceptable?

When the criticism is insulting or demeaning and there is nothing constructive in their feedback, it is neither constructive nor even marginally negative. It may border on a possible personal attack and can originate from a variety of sources, such as the other person's jealousy, insecurity, or guilt. You must remember that you have no control over it, and that even though it is directed at you, it is not about you. When the communication is humiliating or could harm your reputation, it is best to find an objective third party to assist you have a conversation with the offender, as this could be considered bullying. You could be targeted for a variety of reasons:

A supervisor or manager may exert pressure regarding your performance.

You are the person who calls attention to improper conduct.

Your work ethic or standard is preferable to that of your teammate.

The person will intentionally threaten you with injury.

Limits: What, Why, and How

In addition to contacting your human resources department or a therapist to guide you through the process, setting boundaries will assist you.

What Is a Boundary?

It's often difficult for us to set limits on what we're willing to give others because we don't want to cause them harm, but it's crucial that we do so for our own well-being. When someone exceeds your boundaries, you may experience anxiety and distress, which can strain your relationships.

The line that will safeguard you from other people invading your comfort must be drawn through physical contact;

this includes hugging and other forms of contact that allow others to get too close.

Verbal interaction—the manner in which family, acquaintances, and coworkers speak to you.

This determines how near people can stand to you or whether they can enter your home or bedroom when you are not there.

You will set these boundaries based on whether you need to protect yourself emotionally to protect your mental health, if you need to secure your personal space and personal belongings, if your ability to work in tranquility is threatened, or if you need to protect your time from being misused.

When you have exceeded a person's comfort zone, you will typically be aware of this fact without the need for explicit communication. If you verbalize your boundaries to someone who doesn't respect them, it will help to elucidate them.

Why Must We Establish Boundaries?

Everyone has boundaries, but your team member's limits may not be as strict or as lax as yours, which is why it's essential to determine what they are comfortable with. Everyone's boundaries are distinct, and not everyone will comprehend or approve of the limits you've established.

The significance of a boundary is that it prevents you from being physically or emotionally violated. It allows you to take a step back and alert the other person that they are invading your personal space, stating explicitly what you will and will not tolerate within your personal space.

How to Set Healthy Boundaries?

When you've never set clear boundaries for yourself and find it difficult to let others know when they're making you uncomfortable, the best course of action is to determine why you need to establish a limit. The next stage is to determine the type of boundary you need to establish:

This occurs frequently after someone has passed the line with the way they speak to or treat you.

Set up a time to discuss the incident with them.

Recognize when you have done something incorrectly.

Inform them of the unacceptable behavior and politely ask them not to repeat it.

This can be uncomfortable if you prefer people to maintain a certain distance from you or avoid touching you.

Keep your hands near to your body and wave from a small distance.

Do not feel obligated to explain why you prefer not to be touched; simply let them know that you do not wish to be touched.

Do not feel obligated to repent.

This will depend on how you present yourself professionally in the workplace. Deal with a problem as soon as it arises. Wait until after a meeting to communicate with a team member about something they did or said in front of the group.

To protect something you have sacrificed for, it is permissible to set material limits on what you will lend someone and the conditions under which you will do so.

Time limits—one of the most frequently violated boundaries—depend on whether you are consistently late or consistently early.

Determine how long you are willing to wait for someone.

If the time has passed, you are free to cancel the appointment.

If someone is consistently late, let them know that you will only wait for a certain quantity of time.

In the same manner that you may inadvertently violate someone else's boundaries, yours may also be violated. Depending on the gravity of the offense and the sincerity of the contrition, you may decide to sever ties with the offender. This is also acceptable if you have spoken to them about it, either alone or with a mediator, and they continue to do it. This demonstrates a lack of reverence for you as an individual.

You have the right to establish boundaries, and those who care about you will respect them out of concern for your safety. Having these boundaries will also reduce the likelihood of conflict-induced tension.

Forgiveness Throughout and Following the Conflict

When we are in the midst of a conflict, we have a tendency to say and hold on to hurtful things. This becomes bitterness and continues to fuel your wrath, making it difficult to resolve the situation without residual feelings.

During the process, you must determine your motivation for maintaining the tension. Is it a past occurrence that you cannot escape? Is it something the individual did in the past that prevents you from moving on? Because you are at ease with the current state of tension?

Retaining wrath will prolong the conflict, and even if a resolution is reached, the conflict will return because none of the emotions have been resolved. In addition, it will make you resistant to communicating with the other party and unwilling to partake in the process.

Different relationships will determine how we manage conflict and whether or not we are willing to absolve the parties involved. When the relationship is closer, such as with a spouse or coworker, you are more likely to express yourself freely, feel more secure in the situation, and forgive more readily. With those outside your inner circle, your expressions will be more reserved, and you will tend to withdraw from the relationship rather than pursue it.

There will always be emotions associated with the incident, and the more severe the event, such as sexual harassment, the greater the impact on you. The best method to deal with this is to recognize it and find someone to talk to, such as a counselor or therapist.

Method of Forgiveness

To forgive is a deliberate decision to release yourself from the wrath and bitterness caused by a hurtful incident. It provides a new perspective on the incident and prepares you for the act of reconciliation. The act of forgiving a person who has wronged you does not obligate you to have a relationship with that person again. Also, this does not imply that you should wait until the other party asks for your forgiveness, as this may never occur.

Forgiveness is not so much about releasing the offender from the transgression as it is about severing the negative emotions that bind you to the offense.

Why We Refuse to Forgive

You may find it difficult to offer absolution for a variety of reasons, including your fear of appearing vulnerable, the other person's refusal to apologize, your desire to remain a victim, or your lack of support during the process (Kandell, 2012).

Methods for Forgiveness

As with anything else, it is simple to get started on the path to forgiveness if you know the appropriate measures to take:

Acknowledgment—this would include the pain and fury you felt during the incident, as well as the reasons why.

Before making significant decisions, you must give some thought to how the pain is influencing you, including how the person's actions have affected your life.

Acceptance—no matter how angry you are with the person or that the incident occurred, you cannot change it or undo it; it has occurred, and nothing you do can "delete" it from your existence. This phase is necessary for you to determine whether or not it is beneficial to hold onto that anger.

Determination—making the decision to forgive requires deliberation because it will affect how you move forward in relation to the individual, given that the relationship has been irrevocably altered.

Depending on the severity of the incident or the previous toxicity of the situation, you may have the option of attempting to repair the relationship. Restoring the relationship to its former level is not the same as repairing it, because the relationship's dynamic has changed, sometimes for the better and sometimes for the worse. Kindness, compassion, and empathy will be a part of the endeavor to repair the relationship.

Explore - You must take the time to investigate how forgiveness can benefit you more than the other person and how it can help you find serenity to move on from the event with no lingering emotions.

In the majority of cases, you will not verbalize that you have forgiven the individual, and if you do, the response may not be what you anticipated. When you can reflect on the event without experiencing anger or pain, you realize that you can move on, even if you cannot change what occurred.

How to Fight Off Resentment

In every relationship, minor irritations can develop into resentment over time, resulting in a relationship disintegration. To avoid long-term resentment, it is best to communicate them as soon as you become aware of them. There are steps you can take to facilitate your participation in this discussion.

Take note of irritating behaviors; the sooner this occurs, the sooner it can be addressed. What may have seemed like a minor annoyance at the beginning of a relationship, whether personal or professional, can later become a major source of tension and make your work environment extremely uneasy. You must determine what you can tolerate and what will be too much for you.

Look for a calm moment or make an appointment so that you and the individual can have an open conversation about the behavior. This communication must be transparent, and you must also be willing to listen to your teammate.

Be forthright; inform your teammate of your concerns from the outset so that everyone is on the same page. This includes what each individual is accountable for and what you are willing to overlook.

Before communicating with a team member, it is beneficial to discuss your views with a neutral third party. They'll also be able to tell you if you're being reasonable, allowing you to determine if it's something you need to work on by yourself or if it's a legitimate occurrence that you and your colleague need to address jointly. This individual can also be a sounding board for your emotions and a source of calm when you communicate with your teammate.

Remain amenable to negotiation; when conversing with a member of your team, negotiate a compromise, particularly if their actions are causing you harm. Be prepared to hear which of your behaviors they would like to see altered, and negotiate a solution that will make everyone pleased.

Follow through on your commitments; if you've made an agreement with someone, you must honor it without fail. This is something that frequently has difficult relationships.

Be a leader by giving up irritating behaviors that you know irritate the other person. This will encourage them to reflect on their actions and make them more amenable to altering their behavior and more communicative.

Conflict resolution is not only about resolving what is physically manifest, but also about resolving the internal obstacles you and your team must overcome.

Chapter 3: The Hidden Obstacles To Effective Communication And How To Overcome Them

It is difficult to fathom how many obstacles exist between two people in various locations and on different paths. They could be acquaintances, coworkers, business partners, strangers on the street, etc., and they may wish to converse with or connect. However, there are always invisible obstacles in the way, leaving us to ponder why it is so difficult to secure. It's as if two individuals want to communicate something significant but cannot discover a common language. They may wish to, but do not know how. This book focuses on the communication obstacles you encounter when you need to speak with someone immediately and how to overcome them.

What obstacles exist to effective communication?

There are numerous obstacles to effective communication, but one prevents the majority of individuals from even attempting to communicate. They cannot express themselves in a manner that others can hear or comprehend. It is comparable to a linguistic impairment that can be characterized as communication anxiety. It is a feeling of vulnerability and uncertainty associated with approaching others, gaining their attention, and delivering a message so that they comprehend what you want.

You may believe a flaw in your personality causes your communication anxiety, but this is not the case. If you frequently experience these emotions, it is not surprising that you struggle daily with communication. That sensation is the result of how society has been constructed and conditioned, not you. People in our society are afraid of communicating directly and candidly. This is why we use so few words and frequently lack the ability to express ourselves clearly.

Among the invisible obstacles to effective communication are:

The propensity to loose one's identity in a crowd: For instance, someone simultaneously addresses a large group, and no one knows who they are talking about. It is simple for people to lose their identity when conversing with multiple individuals in the same room. People's identities (aspects of themselves or personas) change based on their interactions with others; consequently, they have little chance of knowing and achieving their goals. This can be a problem at work, where individuals cannot state what they want for fear of conflict, looking bad, or being incorrect. This lack of communication abilities is likely to cause issues.

You are expected to initiate action, but you do not: There are numerous instances in which you need to initiate a conversation or say the first word but are unable to. For instance, someone is sitting alone on a park bench while perusing a book, waiting in line at the supermarket or at the bus stop by themselves. It may appear that no one desires to engage in conversation, but consider the situation for a moment. Does it make sense? To develop as individuals, we are all social creatures who seek out interactions with others. We are all essentially identical. We all desire to connect with others, whether for five minutes or eternally.

You fear revealing too much information about yourself: Sometimes, we fear revealing our genuine selves for fear of being deemed offensive. For instance, we explain to others who we are, what we desire, and what drives us. We fear being criticized, reprimanded, or evaluated by others. In order to avoid being rejected or hurt, we typically conceal our true intentions and thoughts about ourselves rather than communicating with others in a humane manner. We fear what others may think of us if they were aware of our thoughts and intentions. It is simpler to keep people at a distance if we do not reveal too much information about ourselves. Instead, we are expected to exhibit a version of ourselves that is less than who we typically are. When we do this, it is difficult to communicate with others.

We lack the ability to be vulnerable. The most important thing you can do if you want to connect with people you care about or routinely interact with is to acknowledge your weakness and ask for assistance. It is the beginning of all communication, much like the origin of communication. It can be learned from a variety of sources, such as psychology, sociology, or simply by observing others, for instance when performing sports, playing the guitar, or dancing. However, many people do not know how to use it effectively when communicating with others. It resembles mother nature. We are all born into the world vulnerable and spend our entire lives learning how to be vulnerable, regardless of race, culture, or heritage.

Fear of conflict may be the greatest barrier to effective communication, as individuals fear confrontation and argument. They wish to speak but fear they will be unable to find the appropriate words, become furious, or say something obnoxious in front of others. Therefore, they avoid discussing significant issues to avoid making a mistake. It is imperative, therefore, to include tactical communication skills in your communication toolkit.

People are hesitant to speak up and share their opinion because they lack confidence and believe that what they have to say may not be appropriate or intriguing enough. They believe others will judge them if they say something incorrect, foolish, or unimportant. Therefore, you must understand what makes people interested in your opinions and how to present them so that people want to attend and comprehend you rather than criticize you.

Lack of interest is another obstacle people encounter when attempting to communicate with others. People do not want to discuss unimportant or uninteresting topics, whether it be their personal or professional problems. In your communication skills training, you must learn how to remove barriers and create meaningful and valuable communication for others.

Chapter 4: What Hinders Your Ability To Communicate Effectively?

Our society has been constructed due to the fact that we are taught to be timid and avoid conflict. It is not how we were raised, but rather how we've been conditioned to think. In certain situations, anxiety can serve as a protective mechanism against potential dangers. Therefore, instead of being upfront and honest with others, we prefer to remain silent so that everyone will know what we want without us having to explicitly state it. However, in other circumstances, terror can be used to control our lives. When conflicts are used as threats to keep us in a lower position in the hierarchy, we are conditioned to believe that we have no choice but to accept the punishment and suffer in silence. If we don't get what we want because someone is obstructing it, then it's time to stop being passive and take matters into your own hands. We are on par with everyone else, so you deserve to get what you desire and require.

Attempting to communicate with others serves no purpose if we cannot be ourselves. We are not the same individuals we were at birth; we develop and change throughout our lives. Instead of attempting to be someone else, we must embrace the person we have become and reside within that person. To communicate effectively, one must be fully present in the moment and not be concerned with what others may perceive. Why would you be concerned about that? It would be ideal if you only concerned about the quality of your interactions with other people.

Your communication style alters your perception of yourself and others. It is as if there is a stratum of glass between you and others, so you cannot perceive what is occurring. Occasionally, you must peer through the lens to see the true picture and comprehend how others perceive it.

The most essential skill in communication is learning how to listen to others, not only for understanding but also for the ability to communicate with them. Does this seem overly simple? It's like comprehending yourself better. You can only comprehend others if you first comprehend yourself. Therefore, when you speak aloud, you must be conscious of what you are saying by observing your behavior, body language, and words, as well as other people's emotions. Otherwise, you will not be able to accomplish the objectives of your communication instruction.

How can invisible barriers to effective communication be overcome?

This is the only question that will be addressed in this book, as it is the most fundamental problem that people encounter when attempting to communicate with others. There is no magic drug that will instantly eliminate barriers and make you an effective communicator. Communication is something that is learned and practiced repeatedly. The good news is that once you learn how to communicate effectively, you will never forget it, and you will use those skills every day.

You will also be able to enhance your communication abilities by learning how to surmount the obstacles that impede and prevent effective communication.

Here are some suggestions for overcoming the intangible obstacles to effective communication:

How do we surmount communication difficulties?

You must first understand how other people communicate. If you are intrigued in someone else, you are more likely to become friends with them if you can comprehend what makes them tick and what drives them. Why is this true? Because comprehending another person facilitates the development of trust between two parties. The greater the faith between two people, the easier it will be for them to connect and establish a meaningful relationship, or, in other words, an eternal friendship.

Become attuned to your own emotions: if you don't know how you feel, how can you possibly interpret the emotions of others? It is essential to be self-aware and learn how to communicate calmly with yourself in order to communicate calmly with others.

Be mindful of the present: You cannot effectively communicate if your mind is elsewhere. You must be entirely present and attentive to what is occurring, who is present, and what they are saying in order to respond to their needs rather than your own. This also applies when speaking with someone over the phone or in person.

Do not fear asking questions: To comprehend someone, you must know what they desire, which requires questioning them. Initially unpleasant and challenging, this is an absolute necessity for effective communication. You must ensure that you listen attentively, that you are interested in what the other person has to say, and that you do not rush through the conversation in order to escape from unpleasant situations or individuals as soon as possible.

Confidence is indispensable: People communicate, interact with others, and feel about themselves in life with confidence. Your communication skills instruction will reveal your lack of self-confidence. Others will be instantaneously attracted to you and want to speak with you if you are optimistic. It is necessary to put yourself out there and become more spontaneous. The more confident and at ease you become, the more effective your communication skills training will be.

Be aware of the topic you wish to discuss: Before beginning the conversation, consider what the other person has to say and the questions you wish to ask them. If you are at a loss for words, try to generate an idea before initiating a conversation. Also, before communicating, attempt to learn more about the person from their words and body language in order to better understand them.

Accepting your emotions is one of the most effective methods for enhancing communication. This involves being in a positive mood, accepting all of your emotions, and being confident in your ability to communicate with others.

If someone is preventing you from attaining something you desire, let go of your fear so you can move forward and accomplish it yourself. Eliminate all obstacles, learn how to handle life situations on your own, and manage your life so that things work out for the best.

Not only is it crucial to hear what others have to say, but learning how to listen makes others feel better because they perceive that you care. You will also be able to communicate more effectively with them if you demonstrate attentiveness.

Do not take things personally; if someone is furious or upset, it is not because of you. People have their own lives and problems, so do not blame yourself for your inability to repair or solve their problems. Accept the circumstances as they are and improve your communication skills instruction.

Flexibility is essential: if people want to communicate in a particular manner, you must accommodate them. If the other person desires a more solemn tone, then adopt that tone. If the other person desires to improve the mood and be happy, you should do the same and be content. It's all about adaptability.

Communication involves being transparent, open, and truthful with one another. Invisible communication barriers are comparable to obstacles that prevent individuals from connecting, communicating, and cooperating. These obstacles are concealed, but they exist nonetheless. If you want to communicate effectively with others, eliminate communication barriers by listening, comprehending, and respecting others. Your instruction in communication skills will bear fruit. In addition, bear in mind the strategies presented in this book for overcoming invisible communication barriers. This will improve your communication with others and in life, as well as your relationship with yourself.

Chapter 5: Body Language

We refer to the nonverbal signals we use to communicate as "body language." We utilize the unspoken aspect of communication to convey our true feelings and give our message more weight. In ordinary conversation, these nonverbal cues play an important role. In fact, body language may account for 60% to 65% of all communication.

When communicating with others, we encrypt our message with a variety of cues that either corroborate our statements or reveal our insincerity (when our words do not reflect our intentions).

There are numerous ways to "see" these signals, such as:

Eye engagement
Hand gestures
Facial expressions

Eye contact is essential to effective communication. It indicates that someone is listening to you and is interested in what you have to say. This is an outstanding example of the icon for attentive listening. It indicates that someone is listening to you and is interested in what you have to say.

This demonstrates outstanding listening skills. If someone won't stare you in the eye, you may not be able to trust them. This causes unease. However, you should be aware that excessive eye contact is considered hostile in some cultures, including Japan and several Middle Eastern countries.

Additionally, gestures can be used to determine a person's actual thoughts and emotions. A person who is truthful and forthright in their words and actions will use "open" gestures, such as extending their arms wide and raising their palms, to demonstrate that they have nothing to hide. Individuals who are feeling uneasy or defensive may be observed shifting laterally, adjusting their collars, touching their nostrils or mouths, crossing their arms, and leaning back (away from you). Examining timepieces and rearranging documents on a desk are two other behaviors that could be construed negatively. By themselves, gestures may be misunderstood. Crossing one's arms is not always an indication of defensiveness; it may also indicate indifference.

Therefore, we should look for motion clusters or groups. For example, a person who leans away from you, has their arms crossed, and avoids eye contact may be concealing something from you.

A salutation is another method of nonverbal communication that we use virtually every day. A handshake may be dominant, subservient, or neutral depending on how the hands are clasped. Hands clasped side by side are impartial.

- Although facial expressions are frequently easy to interpret, they can occasionally be misconstrued.
If the individual's eyes are not involved in the smirk, it is not a smile. Are they truly as engaged as they appear to be, if they have glazed eyes but appear interested? A frown indicates frustration or a lack of comprehension.
Among other things, facial expressions can reveal a person's level of fatigue, health, contentment, or sadness.

Pitch and Tone of the Voice: The pitch and tone of a person's voice can reveal much about their genuine feelings and thoughts. Regardless of the actual words spoken, a person's tone of voice conveys their mental state and receptivity to what is occurring.

intonation refers to the voice's volume, range, and intonation. The greater the frequency of emotion, the higher the intonation (relative to their normal speaking voice). This could be positive, as with enthusiasm and exhilaration, or negative, as with irritation or anger.

Pace of Speech: Another reliable indicator of a person's genuine feelings is their speaking speed. When speech is spoken more rapidly, more emotion is expressed. We must be on the lookout for concentrations of gestures, as this may once again indicate elation or anger. Even if a person speaks swiftly and naturally, they are likely to be unhappy if they have a loud voice and aggressive body language, such as arm gestures that are sweeping.

Chapter 6: A Knowledge Of Body Language

Understanding people's body language enables you to interpret their unspoken emotions and reactions. It is essential feedback, but it can be missed if you do not know what to look for.

Examine the most significant nonverbal cues, some of which have negative connotations and others with positive connotations.

Negative Body Language Examples
If a person exhibits one or more of the following negative behaviors, they are likely disengaged, indifferent, or dissatisfied.

Their limbs are folded in front of their bodies.
Tics or lack of facial expression
Body turned away from you.
Eyes cast downward with minimal eye contact.

These behaviors could be observed when interacting with irate colleagues or dissatisfied customers.

Understanding the significance of these signals will allow you to modify both what and how you communicate. You could, for example, express sympathy for someone's distress, be more forthcoming in your explanations, or attempt to diffuse a tense situation.

If someone exhibits these behaviors during a negotiation, you should concentrate on gaining their attention and putting them at ease. If the negative behavior ceases, you will know they are prepared to deal with you successfully and are more receptive to persuasion. There are additional ways to determine whether someone is tired with your speech. This could take place during a presentation, team meeting, or even a private conversation.

Here are several of the most prevalent indications of boredom:
Slouching while seated and displaying a pessimistic expression.
Staring into space or at other objects.
Confusing pens and phones, Fidgeting and picking at apparel.
Writing or doodling.

Reengaging individuals can be accomplished by posing a direct query or requesting their input.

Nail biting is an indicator of anxiety or tension.
Locked ankles are also related to anxious thoughts.
Blinking rapidly, which may indicate confusion or anxiety.
Sometimes, tapping or drumming the fingers indicates irritation or tedium.
Fidgeting is another indicator of disinterest or preoccupation.

ROLES OF BODY LANGUAGE

In social interactions, body language serves multiple purposes. It can facilitate the following tasks:

It is possible to gain someone's trust by making eye contact, nodding your head in accord while being listened to, or even unintentionally mimicking their body language.

Your message will be received differently depending on the tone of your voice, how you interact with the audience through hand and arm gestures and body language, and the amount of space you occupy.

Truth-telling: When a person's actions do not match their words, we may infer that they are concealing information or are not entirely forthcoming about their emotions.

Putting your own requirements first: Our body language may reveal a great deal about our emotional state. For instance, are you slouched, do you have pursed lips, or is your mandible clenched? This could be an indication that something in your current environment is provoking you. Your body may be communicating that you feel apprehensive, unsafe, or any number of other emotions.However, bear in mind that your interpretation of another person's body language may not always be accurate.

Chapter 7: How To Improve Your Physical Presentation

The first step in developing your body language is to pay attention. Test your ability to recognize the bodily cues of others, in addition to your own. You may have a tendency to look down while someone is relating a story to you. Try making eye contact and even smiling to demonstrate that you are engaged in the conversation. Finding equilibrium is the key to using body language effectively.

For example, seizing a person's hand firmly prior to a job interview may convey professionalism. However, if you grasp it too tightly, the other person may be injured or annoyed. Always consider how others might be feeling.

Additionally, continue to develop your emotional intelligence. The greater your awareness of your own emotions, the simpler it is to discern how others perceive you. You will be able to determine whether someone is open and receptive or closed off and in need of space. If we wish to induce a specific emotion, we may use our body language.

STARTERS OF CONVERSATION ICEBREAKERS

Asking ice-breaker questions is a fun and engaging way to get to know someone and to keep a conversation continuing.

These are some examples of icebreakers:
What are you currently reading?
Who would you choose and why, if you could meet any historical figure, living or deceased, and why?
What film did you just view?
What did you appreciate or dislike about it?

If you could learn anything, what would you learn first?What is your greatest book?
What is your fave film?
Which of your previous trips was the most memorable?
Which superpower would you most like to possess?Have you ever attained a personal objective?
Have you any collections?
What would you do with the extra hour if there were 25 hours in the day?
Which song is your fave for karaoke?
Which animal, and why, would you choose to be if given the opportunity?
Which celebrities do they resemble, in your opinion?
What is the most unusual cuisine you've ever eaten?
Do you have a specific source of motivation for your work?
What is the most valuable piece of career advice you have ever received?
What is your favorite indoor activity?
Which location would you like to visit next?

SUBJECTS/Topics to Avoid

When learning how to engage in conversation with others, one of your first queries will be, "What are interesting topics to discuss?" However, it is essential to know which topics to avoid when conversing with strangers.

As a general rule, avoid:
Elicit a debate about politics
Discuss religion
Sexual issues and intimate relationships are discussed.
Provide excessive detail about a disease or injury.
Discuss your personal finances, including money, wages, and benefits.
Regarding demographics such as age, controversy, a specific gender or ethnicity, etc., make broad statements.

When you have established a rapport with the other person, you may discuss these topics, but you should avoid them initially.

The objective is to avoid contentious exchanges that have the potential to anger others. When you initiate a delightful conversation with a stranger, coworker, or colleague, you may develop a strong bond.

Chapter 8: Developing Expertise In Non-Verbal Communication

Consider having a conversation with a colleague in the office cafeteria. She is conversing with you while fidgeting with her phone and avoiding eye contact. Do you believe she is listening to what you have to say, or is she simply killing time until she must return to work?

Every time you speak, roughly half of your message is conveyed through your words. The remaining half consists of nonverbal cues such as your tone of voice, facial expressions, posture, and gestures. People will not believe you if your nonverbal cues do not support your point of view, regardless of what you say. Consider the preceding example; the disinterested colleague may be completely engaged in her conversation with you, but her body language indicates otherwise. Even if you are aware that you are giving someone your undivided attention, they will not realize it if you gaze down at your shoes, turn away from them, or fiddle with your phone or keys. No one enjoys conversing with an uninterested individual.

Then, are you able to correlate your message with your body language? Can you regulate your gestures and expressions on your face? Can you convey interest and concentration to the person with whom you are conversing? Yes, you can readily align your body language with your speech in each of the situations listed above. However, would it feel forced? Can people detect when you're attempting to smile and make eye contact too hard? If you know how to effectively employ body language, the answer is no.

First recommendation: maintain eye contact.

Consider the frequency of the word "eyes" in everyday phrases and idioms. A romantic interest may have "bedroom eyes," which is slang for being unreliable. A person you care about could be described as the "apple of your eye." In competitions, it is recommended to keep one's "eyes on the prize." The proverb "the eyes are the windows to the soul" has been heard by nearly everyone.

To solicit feedback, individuals engage in eye contact. When posing a query or pausing the conversation, we frequently look someone in the eye unconsciously. At grammatical pauses and the end of sentences, we look into one another's eyes to "pass the baton," so to speak, and invite the other to participate. Eye contact is also utilized as a synchronization technique. Eye contact is essential for effective communication because it demonstrates curiosity, honesty, and integrity.

With practice, making appropriate eye contact with another person can be as simple as gazing through a window, despite the intimidating psychology underlying it. In a sense, you are gazing through a window into another person's thoughts and emotions. Simply consider the following:

First, make eye contact. Even if a person appears unresponsive, do not be afraid to stare them in the eye. It is possible that the individual you are speaking with feels similarly awkward making eye contact. Therefore, you should not interpret a person's lack of eye contact as an indication of disinterest. Simply attempt again after a brief delay.

But avoid gazing. If you make two attempts at eye contact and the other person does not respond, you should give up. Again, it is possible that they are unable to make eye contact, so you shouldn't presume they don't want to speak with you. This is particularly important to keep in mind when conversing with a foreigner, as various cultures have different standards for eye contact.

Determine when you should turn your gaze. It is essential to maintain eye contact with your target, but it is equally important not to fixate your entire body on them. Too much eye contact can appear hostile and even frightening. Every few seconds, shift your gaze to a different portion of the other individual's body or visage. After a few seconds, reestablish eye contact.

In addition to maintaining eye contact, employ additional nonverbal communication techniques. Lean back when making eye contact with someone you do not know well to show that you respect their privacy. If they are discussing something private or significant, lean slightly closer. This will demonstrate your willingness to listen to their opinions.

Avoid making eye contact your primary concentration. Focus your attention on a shared interest when conversing, and observe your surroundings when walking. It is normal to glance away from the individual you are speaking with every few seconds.

Appears to be much to recall? While conversing with someone, practice maintaining eye contact by focusing on one eye for three seconds, the other eye for three seconds, and then their lips for three seconds. Every few seconds, look aside from their face for three seconds. Rather than mentally counting down the seconds, estimate the time. As a consequence, you will be able to make eye contact more naturally.

It may be advantageous to slightly raise your eyebrows when gazing someone in the eye. This facilitates your ability to maintain a neutral but engaged facial expression. Some people experience drooping eyebrows during conversations, giving the impression that they are sad or scowl. Take a deep breath, raise your eyebrows, or slightly open your eyes (without making a "shocked" expression) and then resume eye contact.

Chapter 9: Genuinely Smile To Make Others Feel Distinguished.

Although eye contact and other nonverbal signals can vary between cultures, a smile is universal. It represents universal friendship, acceptance, and generosity. Additionally, it is automatic; no effort is required to smile when hearing or seeing something pleasurable. Obviously, you may grin whenever you please. However, if done improperly, a forced smile appears to be artificial.

Imagine a gathering in which some people are sincerely happy while others are not. Every time, it is simple to identify the forced smiles because they appear strained rather than joyous and carefree. Some individuals compensate for this by making inappropriate facial expressions, while others choose not to smile if they feel compelled to do so. Who is enjoying themselves and who is simply going through the motions can always be distinguished.

There is no need to appear to be forcing your smile. Have you ever witnessed the cashier in a store smiling at the customers? Through hundreds, if not thousands, of client interactions, he has cultivated a smile that appears effortless and natural. However, you do not need to interact with hundreds, thousands, or even dozens of people to develop the same natural, sincere smile. Please remember these suggestions.

Your grin extends past your jaw. When you smile spontaneously, your cheekbones swell, your eyes sparkle, and your nose wrinkles slightly. If you only move your mouth into a smile without moving the rest of your face, your smile will appear forced and unnatural.

Find something amusing (such as a YouTube video or the memory of a favored joke) and practice smiling in front of a mirror. Take note of how your smile fills your entire visage. After that, attempt to relax and smile. See the difference?

One need only smile with their gaze. You can smile without opening your mouth if you practice giving your irises a smile-like appearance. While beaming in front of a mirror, conceal the lower half of your face and focus on your eyes.

Practice adjusting your eyes to achieve a similar result without beaming.

Experience leads to perfection. In front of a mirror, practice your smile by grinning for ten seconds, allowing it to expand for ten more, and repeating. Perform this exercise daily. Developing and toning the facial muscles similarly to other muscles can make your smile appear more natural.

Learn both when and how to smile. Obviously, nobody always smiles. A sincere smile lasts approximately the same amount of time as genuine eye contact, between three and five seconds. Additionally, some individuals are anxious laughers; they smile and laugh to alleviate their discomfort in awkward or uncomfortable situations. However, doing so can be perceived as inappropriate, so if you find yourself beaming when no one else is, maintain a neutral facial expression. Try to smile when the person you are conversing with beams, but refrain from smiling back, as they may notice if you don't.

Develop Your Body Language Competence

Eye contact and smiling are only two examples of body language. There are a variety of additional nonverbal means by which individuals may express their thoughts, emotions, and mental state. Initially, the features Imagine you are conversing with your neighbor when she mentions a person or place that you do not recognize. You may observe a small furrow between your eyebrows or a minor lateral tilt of your head. This may reveal to your neighbor that you did not fully comprehend what she said, giving her the opportunity to elaborate. If she does not, you may ponder about "Linda from Harlingen" for the duration of the conversation. You can see how crucial it is in this situation to interpret nonverbal cues. If the roles were reversed, you wouldn't want your neighbor to query who or what you are discussing.

Consider a situation that is more formal, such as the workplace. In a meeting with your supervisor to discuss your performance, sitting cross-legged, keeping your hands close to your body, making few facial movements, and avoiding eye contact may make you appear defensive. Your supervisor may be mystified as to why you feel the need to defend yourself; are you concerned about your own subpar performance on the job? Have you anything to hide from him? How would you respond to the defensive body language of another if the roles were reversed?

It is essential to be able to read and interpret body language, but anyone can acquire this skill. In general, a person is receptive and approachable when their body is facing you and their limbs are at their sides. They are also "closed off" if they turn away from you, cross their legs, fold their arms across their chest, or otherwise place distance between you and them to communicate that they do not wish to speak with you.

On a scale, body language indicators typically fall between comfortable and uneasy. Comfortable body language includes eye contact, expansive gestures, an upright posture, smiles, and relaxed conversation. Uncomfortable body language includes crossed legs and arms, a slouched posture, averting eye contact, and muted or artificial speech. Obviously, you will feel positive about the conversation if you observe relaxed body language. However, if you observe apprehensive body language, you should determine the source of their discomfort. Here are some additional common motions and how to interpret them:

Touching the chin with a finger, slightly tilting the head, shifting the gaze to an unknown location while listening, and sustaining eye contact while speaking. Considering what is being said to them before responding is likely the topic of discussion here. This is a common practice of interviewers. Allow the other person ample time to respond to your direct inquiries, demonstrating your interest and concern for their response.

Avoiding eye contact, modifying vocal pitch, perspiring, and exhaling more heavily than usual. This individual may be telling falsehoods. After they have finished speaking, ask them precise questions to determine whether you should believe them.

Pallor, stuttering, voice quivering, fidgeting, and blushing were observed. In this instance, the subject may be anxious or agitated. If your topic of conversation appears to be causing their anxiety, try asking them questions to determine their concerns or changing the subject.

This is by no means an exhaustive list of body language indicators, as the use of body language by individuals and cultures varies. Some of the telltale indications of dishonesty are not always present; instead, a person may exhibit nervous behavior. Like establishing eye contact and smiling, practice is necessary. Observe how others communicate and compare their words with their actions. Pay attention to your own behavior when you communicate. You will eventually acquire an understanding of nonverbal signals that will allow you to interpret and even influence everyday situations.

Chapter 10: Who Are Intelligent Negotiators?

Intelligent negotiators are well-prepared, assured, and highly efficient. They are familiar with each phase of a negotiation session. They have established their own objectives and determined the most effective means of achieving them; they are also aware of the objectives of their competitors. Intelligent negotiators utilize their extensive knowledge of negotiation processes to devise effective negotiation strategies that advance their side's interests while enhancing the final outcome for all parties.

Frequently, the Intelligent Negotiator's objectives are work-related. Who will cover the Omaha client meeting? Should we charge the standard 10% commission on a contract with a specific client, or should we reduce it to 7% or

8% to ensure future client loyalty? What quality assurances should we anticipate from the potential raw material supplier? Should I demand the executive title of the person I'm replacing, or should I wait until I've demonstrated my competence?

Sometimes, negotiation is a personal or professional matter. How can I obtain the ideal position that has just become available? How can I receive the salary I was originally promised? How can I obtain the raise I believe I deserve? Can I convince my supervisor to change the negative comments on my most recent performance evaluation? How can I communicate with my colleagues and subordinates more effectively?

Family and quality of life are two additional significant factors. What plans does our family have for the summer? Can we obtain a second mortgage with more favorable terms to fund our child's college expenses? How can we minimize the cost of automobile and appliance maintenance? Negotiation is the key to determining the optimal solution in each of the aforementioned situations.

Even if we are unaware of it, everyone negotiates their way through existence. We negotiate on a daily basis with family, friends, neighbors, business partners, salesmen, and total strangers. However, many of us are uncomfortable with the concept of negotiating. We fear the psychological battle of wills, as well as the rituals of exploitation and lies that frequently accompany it. We tell ourselves that negotiation is rare and that the majority of things are not negotiable. We visit stores, inspect the price tags of desired items, and determine whether or not to purchase them at the listed prices. We seldom pursue better terms because we are terrified of seeming dumb if we do. If only we realized how many salespeople in even the most conservative retail establishments are willing to negotiate lower prices or other customer-beneficial agreements when asked, we could learn a great deal.

Sometimes, businesspeople underestimate the extent to which they must negotiate with their superiors, subordinates, and peers. They structure work connections, supplier contracts, and customer interactions erratically, oblivious to the bargaining qualities — and potential advantages — of these vital links.

Some less skilled negotiators justify their lack of interest in the bargaining process by stating that the price or value of the vast majority of commercial and noncommercial items is determined by objective market forces. They feel powerless to influence "externally regulated" matters. This assumption entirely disregards the always subjective personal factors that influence negotiations. If a prospective buyer desires a popular automobile model or property, he or she will almost certainly pay a premium. Alternatively, someone eager to purchase a different automobile or home may offer a lower price, potentially saving thousands of dollars. Those with new employment offers who negotiate for a higher starting salary earn significantly more than those who accept the initial offers. Even department store consumers who negotiate prices can save 10 to 20 percent compared to those who pay the listed prices. Those who respectfully inquire, "Is this the best price you can offer me?" may receive the previous week's sale price or a discount if they purchase two of the items under consideration.

Skilled negotiators understand that factors other than the fundamental selling price have a substantial impact on bargaining sessions. These various factors define the settlement range (see figure 1). As each party prepares for a negotiation, its players analyze the relevant objective considerations, such as the monetary cost of specific items, the opportunity costs of changing jobs, and the value of anything else that could be exchanged for other benefits. Comparable calculations are made by the opposing side with regard to the pertinent objects. Each party determines the amount that it is willing to pay or accept in order to partake in the proposed transaction. The settlement range is determined by the intersection of the parties' bottom lines (illustrated by the dark region in Figure 1). Both negotiators concur on all range-related issues.

As soon as the parties begin to negotiate and enter the settlement range, objective factors vanish and subjective elements begin to influence party behavior. How much do both parties want the agreement? The level of risk-taking or risk aversion possessed by each individual. A mental conflict of wills is occurring within the settlement range. If one side can persuade the other that they must take the same course of action, the other side will do so. Due to the numerous subjective factors that influence interactions, individuals agree to vastly different terms for ostensibly comparable transactions. As a negotiation consultant, I was involved in a personal-injury debate many years ago. The client was injured, and his counsel sought $100,000 in compensation from the insurance company. After rejecting that amount, the plaintiff decided to retain the services of the attorney with whom I am affiliated. We negotiated aggressively and resolved the $100,000 lawsuit for more than $500,000! Our efforts were beneficial to the plaintiff, but costly to the insurance company, which should have recognized the legitimacy of the initial $100,000 claim and taken swift action.

Those who comprehend the fundamental concepts underlying all interpersonal interactions outperform those who do not. They are aware of how to prepare for these conversations, the importance of verbal and nonverbal communication skills, and the variety of bargaining tactics used. They understand when to be resolute and when to be more accommodating.

Skillful negotiation enables you to create opportunities for yourself and your negotiation companions. We are conversing with those on the opposite side of the table because they are able to assist us. Both parties believe that a successful agreement will enhance their current circumstances. Relationships will flourish if superiors and subordinates can concur on work assignments and performance goals. Those who purchase and sell products and services will benefit from establishing trustworthy relationships. Their relationships will deteriorate if they are unable to reach an accord on their multiple interconnected problems.

One of my most recent negotiations demonstrates the value of bargaining alternatives. I arrived in Atlanta and checked into the hotel where my reservation was confirmed. The attendant stated that he was out of space due to an abnormally high number of late-departing customers. He offered to relocate me to a different hotel, but I asked if any were vacant. He claimed to have a studio apartment with a solitary bed. This was acceptable to me, but the $175 cost for the motel I had reserved was excessive for the amenities provided. I remained silent as I awaited his response. I expected a reasonable price reduction and was astonished when he offered me the smaller room at no cost. I'm glad I didn't make the initial offer because I would have suggested between $100 and $120!

Chapter 11: The Ritualistic Nature Of Negotiating

The majority of people dislike the ritualistic nature of bargaining encounters. Why don't negotiators communicate their true feelings? Why do they have to engage in deceptive games that appear to be designed to exploit others? Why do we waste so much time debating apparently insignificant subjects like traffic, weather, sports, politics, and shared friends before delving into the heart of the matter? Why can't we just say up front what we want and what we're ready to give up to get those things?

Most negotiating agreements have ritualistic components for a number of reasons. Individuals feel nervous when they begin a negotiation interaction, even while dealing with friends or acquaintances. They have no notion whether peaceful negotiations can be achieved, or what boundaries will be agreed upon. If both parties begin stressed, they may encounter difficulties that may prohibit them from reaching an agreement. By taking the time to build rapport and establish a more favorable negotiation environment, they significantly boost the probability of a pleasant and productive dialogue.

Smith Williams, a negotiation expert and law professor at Brigham Young University, spent several years in Afghanistan, where all consumer goods are negotiable. He was forced to barter for fruits and vegetables, meat and poultry, bread, and other basics. He repeated the process with the potato seller, asking, "How much are the potatoes?" He was told they were 12 per kilogram. He said that they did not seem to be in good health and offered two. The merchant reacted with a ten, Smith retorted with a four, the merchant countered with an eight, and Smith countered with a six, which was accepted.

Smith chose to forego this ceremony and instead pay 6 for his potatoes. He came early and saw a woman do the typical 12, 2, 10, 4, 8, and 6 transactions. He then ordered a kilo of potatoes and placed 6 on the counter. According to the dealer, they were 12. When Smith mentioned that he had been paying 6 for weeks, the merchant replied that potato prices had increased owing to a drought in the North. Smith then told the merchant about the 6 sales to the woman in front of him, but he was assured that it was a "mission of mercy." That woman had just lost her husband and was fighting to support her children. A large number of little children. As a consequence, he lost money on the transaction.

Smith spent the most time with the merchant that day, and he left empty-handed. The merchant declined to sell for Smith's original offer of 6 since it would be an insult, and Smith refused to pay more than 6. "How much are the potatoes?" Smith inquired the following morning. Smith recognized the importance of ritualistic behavior in negotiating situations.

The parties evaluate one another at the early stage of a bargaining session. Each party is interested in learning about the other party's personal and professional background, negotiating experience, external opportunities that may be available to the other party, and the degree to which the items being exchanged are required. Individuals who ignore the importance of these early conversations risk supplying their opponents with vital information that they may later use against them.

When you engage in the negotiating process, allow it to grow gradually. Recognize that it may take some time for apprehensive participants to feel at comfortable in these sessions. Negotiators who are impatient are cursed twice. Surprisingly, the quicker they debate something, the longer it takes. The stages do not work and must be repeated. Furthermore, because of a lack of cooperative bargaining, the more eager negotiators hurry a negotiation session, the less effective the distribution of the goods being exchanged will be. Patient negotiators who allow the process to develop gradually get faster and better results overall.

The persistent dishonesty involved in bargaining is the second irritating feature. Someone who is willing to pay $21,000 on a car does not initiate contact with the seller by announcing this figure, nor does the salesman who is perfectly content to sell the vehicle for $19,800 mention that price right away. The buyer and seller engage in an awkward dance in which one tries to convince the other to disclose a certain monetary number. The salesperson emphasizes the sticker price of $22,500, while the potential client mentions the dealer cost of $19,000. After a seeming never-ending exchange of incremental concessions, the parties agree on a price in the $20,000 to $20,500 range that meets both parties' underlying objectives. Regardless of the fact that although it would have made the exchange more joyful and less stressful if the parties had agreed on this price from the beginning, most participants are unable to do so. They must understand that without the ritualistic testing of each side's resolve and the preceding disclosure of misleading attitudes, the buyer cannot determine how low the dealer is willing to go and the salesperson cannot forecast how much the buyer is willing to pay. Those who ignore the bargaining aspects of such a contract are likely to pay their $21,000 limit—and some may be convinced to pay $500 to $1,000 extra.

Have they engaged in atrocious deception when the automobile salesperson starts the initial discussion by saying, "I cannot go lower than the

$22,500 sticker price," and the prospective buyer begins by saying, "I will not go beyond the $19,000 dealer cost"? Most people who properly research this topic are likely to respond "no." An honest person does not always say the truth, but rather discloses the truth when it is expected. Most of us would not consider it dishonest to compliment a colleague's new outfit or hairstyle even if we did not think it was attractive, or to falsely notify an acquaintance that we had another engagement when asked to a dinner we would like to skip. We understand that an honest response may be seen as unduly harsh.

When we deal, certain dishonesty is expected, especially when we are involved in commercial talks or company activities. Each side tries to convince the other that it must give more lenient terms than are required to conclude the deal. As a result, we don't anticipate totally candid responses to cost or value issues. We anticipate some "puffing" and "embellishment," as long as the statements do not deviate too far from reality. We expect car dealers to emphasize sticker prices, and salespeople to assume that experienced buyers will prioritize dealer costs. Both will be unwilling to go much higher or lower than these standards. The salesman will emphasize the vehicle's sophisticated sound system's $1,000 retail price (which actually cost the dealer $600), while the potential customer will deceptively show little interest in such a pricey feature. So long as these inaccuracies concern our actual settlement plans and the value we place on the various

As products are exchanged, deception will be permitted. Claims of dishonesty emerge only when the misrepresentations affect subjects about which we have a right to know. For example, if a car salesperson said that a vehicle had side air bags when it just had front air bags, or that a six-cylinder engine had eight cylinders, such misrepresentations would be considered unethical, if not fraudulent.

Intelligent negotiators can recognize the difference between expected puffing and exaggeration and unethical lying. They appreciate the critical role that personal integrity plays in their ability to effectively negotiate. The vast majority of negotiating transactions are conducted orally, in person, or over the phone, with parties relying on the factual information provided. People's bargaining power would suffer greatly if they lost their reputation for honesty when it was needed. Everything they stated had to be confirmed, and all agreements had to be documented and signed in writing. Bargaining would become inefficient and time-consuming. If you ever contemplate openly lying about important facts, evaluate how such deception may affect your future encounters if detected.

Reading this book will teach you the precise phases and strategies of the bargaining process. The first part discusses what you must do before sitting down to eat: Understand which negotiating strategy to use, establish your bottom line, assess your counterpart's bargaining power, set firm ambition levels for yourself, prepare your first offer, and plan the sequence of events.

The second half shows how to build rapport, create value, and claim value throughout the periods when players appraise one another, give basic information, and determine who gets what. You will learn how to obtain information about the other party's personal and professional background, bargaining experience, external options that they may have, and the degree to which the goods being exchanged are required. You'll also learn how to shape the pie, defend your arguments as forcefully as possible, plan your concession strategy, and cope with various negotiating ploys.

The final section includes hundreds of negotiating tactics, methods to firmly fulfill the agreement, and strategies to extend the pie with cooperative bargaining in order to maximize the results provided by the bargaining parties.

The last section provides practical applications of negotiation strategies for job offers, acquiring automobiles and residences, and dealing with repair shops.

Because of your significant educational history, you may believe you are already an excellent negotiator, or you may be concerned that you are an inept bargainer due to a lack of formal education. In over thirty years of teaching negotiation courses, practicing law, and resolving conflicts, I have discovered no association between negotiating competence and educational achievement. Successful academics and great negotiators demand a variety of mental abilities. Higher IQ levels indicate that successful students have good abstract thinking ability, but effective negotiators have superior interpersonal skills, or what brain researcher and consultant Daniel Goleman refers to as emotional intelligence. 1 Intelligent Negotiators are aware of how to prepare for negotiating exchanges, the significance of verbal and nonverbal communication skills, and the many games that are played.

My goal is to help you acquire the skills needed to become a more competent negotiator. When you understand the stages and use the methods, you will notice that every negotiation, whether personal, professional, or organizational, seems to you to be unique. Negotiations will be more pleasant, and you will be thankful that they offer opportunity for both you and your opponents.

Jasmine and Philip Brown are in their early thirties. They have two children, a seven-year-old boy and a five-year-old daughter, and have been married for 10 years. Philip and Susan originally met 11 years ago.

Jasmine was a high school science teacher in Smallville. Philip quit teaching four years ago to take a scientific post at the State Environmental Protection Agency office in Smallville, where he now earns $52,000 per year. Jasmine received her Master's Degree in computer science and network administration three years ago and has since been teaching computer science classes to eleventh and twelfth grade students. She has also helped with the management of her school district's computer network. She is currently paid $42,000 per year.

Philip has been assigned to the State Environmental Protection Agency in Metropolis, the state capital. His salary would increase to $57,000, enabling him and Jasmine to relocate closer to both sets of parents, who live in Metropolis suburbs. Jasmine had considered leaving teaching to work as a network manager for a small retail company in the Metropolis area. If Philip and Jasmine decide to relocate, Jasmine must get a job offer from one of the several retail firms who are presently hiring network managers and negotiate her new working terms.

Chapter 12: Manage And Pro-Actively

The initial stage is to be proactive and take charge of the negotiation process. To map out the issues, create an agenda that will help you reach an agreement that meets your objectives. Try to be truthful with yourself when choosing or concurring on what they are. Remember that pricing is only one aspect of the transaction and that winning on price alone might not result in the best deal. You may require cooperation to the extent that the other party not only agrees to move forward but is also eager to do so.

Recognize their commitment. Your vanity has no place in your conversations. The only factor that matters is the agreement's total value over its duration.

Selling vs. negotiating

It is commonly assumed that a successful "sell" will close on its own and that negotiation will only occur when there are substantial differences. However, negotiating as a talent and practice is fundamentally distinct from selling. To sell is to emphasize the advantages and match the solution to the need. Explanation, justification, and a logical argument are required. The phrase "the gift of the gab" refers to a salesperson who responds enthusiastically to every inquiry. Negotiation is ineffective. Although connections are essential, as is an atmosphere conducive to collaboration (without which there can be no discourse), the behavior of a Completely

Skilled Negotiator also includes appropriate silence. This involves listening to what the other individual says, recognizing what they don't say, and determining their true perspective.

Silence

Before responding, silence enables you to ponder and reflect. It enables you to truly comprehend the opposing viewpoint by permitting you to listen. Discipline and vigilance are necessary. The disconcerting effect of silence is that the opposing party continues to speak and ultimately makes unanticipated concessions. Frequently, they provide you with more information than they intended.

Negotiation requires planning, questioning, listening, and making proposals, as well as recognizing when the selling phase has concluded and the negotiation phase has begun. If you find yourself selling the benefits of your proposals during a negotiation, you are likely demonstrating vulnerability and ceding control. It implies that you do not consider your proposals to be sufficiently robust and that they require further promotion. The more you communicate, the more likely you are to concede. Recognizing when the transaction has shifted from selling to negotiating is crucial. You are now in negotiations. Practicing patience makes it simple to remain silent, observe, and reflect. Since you are currently negotiating, this silence may feel awkward.

PERSONAL ETHICS

Fairness, honesty, integrity, and trust all naturally inspire us to be hospitable. In every relationship, personal values play a role, but corporate partnerships can and frequently do exist on the basis of distinct value systems. Many individuals are sensitive when their values are questioned, as if their fundamental integrity were being brought into question. The crucial point is that they are neither right nor wrong. I am not suggesting that effective negotiators lack values; we all possess them. However, when participating in a negotiation, what you do and what you say do not need to be identical. This is not intended to challenge who you are, but rather to assist you in altering your behavior.

Throughout a negotiation, there is nothing incorrect with maintaining your integrity. Others, however, may not be as dedicated to theirs, leaving you susceptible. In other words, if you choose to be open and honest with another person, such as by providing them with information, and they choose not to reciprocate, guess who obtains the upper hand? And how appropriate is that?

Where natural economic processes, such as supply and demand, cause individuals to conduct business with one another, a cooperative connection may help to expand opportunities but is not required. Trust and integrity are excellent corporate values because they are defendable and secure, especially when hundreds or thousands of people are purchasing or selling on behalf of a business. They also facilitate the development of long-term business relationships. However, the same principles may lead to complacency, familiarity, and even sloth in negotiations, all of which cost shareholders money. I continue to believe in collaborative partnerships, but with an emphasis on maximizing value and ensuring the best interests of all parties.

Justification for Collaboration

It is possible that you favor collaborative negotiating because: • You need the other party's commitment and drive to deliver on your agreement; • you prefer to work within a set of variables that allows you to consider all of the implications and total value at stake; • you believe it is a more effective way to manage relationships; or • you fear conflict and the potential negative consequences of the negotiation failing.

Regardless of your motivation, ensure that it is based on the likelihood that it will help you achieve your goals, as opposed to a simple preference for a comfortable environment. It depends on how truthful you are with yourself regarding your motivations and the benefits of collaboration.

Chapter 13: Conflict Management And Difficult Dialogue

If we yield to our peer groups or upbringing, we are not consciously selecting how to resolve disagreements. When we are genuine and compassionate, and make self-responsible, autonomous decisions that are allowing and nurturing, we can resolve disagreements constructively and with love. As we exemplify the characteristics associated with being genuine and loving, growing in character, and gaining knowledge, we are empowered to make better decisions as we seek the one right decision that will resolve the issue in the most advantageous fashion for all parties involved.

The preponderance of our disagreements with our children stem from the fact that we are still maturing as parents. Conflicts increase as we become less sincere and courteous. Parents cause conflict by controlling, judging, lying, personalizing behavior, acting disrespectfully, reacting instead of choosing a response, believing they own their children, and failing to venerate, appreciate, or attempt to comprehend them. When parents conduct in this manner, their children may become aggressive, rebellious, resentful, angry, disobedient, sad, feel unloved, and have a low sense of self-worth, resulting in behavioral problems at home, in the community, and in the classroom. Interestingly, when this occurs, parents frequently seek explanations from other sources, such as their children's schools, peers, the media, or other parents. They will attribute their children's problems to lyrics from violent songs and violent television programs. Due to their inability to embrace responsibility, these parents frequently assign blame to parties other than their children.

They defend themselves by claiming they adore their children, even though this may not be the case.

As a result, we frequently need to reprimand our children in order to resolve issues that we caused. As we continue to cause conflict, it typically escalates and intensifies. In the worst-case scenario, parents may give up in contempt and abandon their children to fend for themselves, physically abuse their children, or permanently expel older students. This behavior pattern may continue to spiral and repeat. Other times, children make their own decisions to leave, or they act out the conflicts they observe in their environment, causing harm to others or getting deeper into trouble.

On the other hand, the more compassionate and genuine we are, the less likely we are to engage in conflict. If we lived by these values from the moment our children were born, they would imitate our behavior and realize their inherent goodness.

They would be considerate, patient, cooperative, pensive, loving, self-motivated, and deeply invested in the world around them. Even if we were not prepared to declare them saints, they would still be joyful, fulfilled, independent, trustworthy, and loving.

If we wait until our children are nearly adults before deciding to be genuine and affectionate, we face a formidable obstacle. Since the birth of our offspring, we have not embodied the corresponding characteristics and values, and as a result, we have generated and continue to generate conflict. We struggle to strike a balance between our need for immediate conflict resolution and our desire for more favorable long-term results. As we strive to improve ourselves and reduce conflict with our children, we must make decisions about the most effective means of resolving these disagreements.

How to have sensitive conversations with your child may be a difficult aspect of nurturing their lives. a horrible incident like 9/11. a family member passing away. Mom and Dad have separated. Multiple factors make it challenging to discuss these interactions: Parents may struggle to maintain emotional control. It may be challenging to know what to say. And many people fear that discussing a problematic subject will only exacerbate the issue.

These principles may serve as a guide when discussing challenging topics with your children:

They are more intelligent than you believe

The majority of children have extraordinary sensitivity to sensitive information. Consider the likelihood that your child has observed your body language and heard conversations about which she has already formed opinions.

Nowadays, children have access to a multitude of media outlets. Your child has almost undoubtedly seen or heard something about it if recordings from 9/11 are circulating on the anniversary of the tragedy or if another disturbing event is making headlines.

2. Keep it regulated

Children feel apprehensive when a caregiver overcommunicates or undercommunicates in response to anything. Some parents provide their children with more information than they can emotionally or cognitively comprehend in order to keep the lines of communication open. Communication is the opposite extreme of the spectrum. On the opposite extreme of the spectrum, parents view difficult topics as taboo and avoid discussing them.

The child is then left to work through complex issues, consider the repercussions, and attempt to fill in knowledge gaps where necessary.

3. heed your child's counsel.

Due to the fact that every child is unique, the optimal strategy is to cater to their individual needs. She may be eavesdropping on conversations between adults. Observe a change in conduct or an increase in anxiety? Is he attentively viewing the news on television? Typically, these are signs that he requires knowledge and emotional support. Use these queries to elicit your child's inquiries. Give straightforward, sincere, and succinct responses, and then keep an eye out for verbal or nonverbal signals that the conversation has provided him with the information and solace he requires.

4. Reconciliate Feelings

When adults respond with statements such as "I can see it makes you very depressed," "You are sad because you won't be able to see your father as often," or "That news story made me sad as well," they contribute to establishing a stable environment for their children in trying or unpleasant circumstances. When sentiments are acknowledged, respected, and valued, your child's relationship with his or her family improves dramatically.

Chapter 14: Identifying And Resolving Conflict Origins

Parenting necessitates open communication even more than other relationships. When we communicate with our children, we can build trust, foster comprehension, and strengthen our bond with them. Nonetheless, disagreements will inevitably arise. To effectively manage these conflicts, it is essential to identify and address their root causes.

Finding the source of the conflict is a crucial first step in resolving disagreements with your child.

This may be challenging because disagreements can involve a variety of issues, such as misinterpretations, poor communication, and divergent principles or goals. To find a solution that satisfies everyone, it may be beneficial to determine the root cause of the problem.

One way to determine the underlying cause of a disagreement is by asking yourself and your child open-ended questions that promote investigation and comprehension. For instance, you may inquire as to what is troubling your child or what they deem to be the most significant problem. If you give your child the opportunity to express their thoughts and feelings, you can gain a deeper understanding of his or her perspective and the reasons for the disagreement.

Consideration of your role in the situation is an additional crucial step in resolving the fundamental issue. Accepting responsibility for your actions and acknowledging any mistakes you may have made can help reduce tension and find a solution when disagreements arise.

Let's use a real-world illustration to illustrate these concepts. Imagine that you have a strict curfew for your child and that he or she is upset about it. Your child may believe that retiring to bed at a particular time is unfair or that they are being treated differently than their siblings. In this instance, identifying the source of the disagreement is crucial.

Ask your child why he or she believes bedtime is unjust, and pay close attention to his or her response. This will help you understand their perspective and identify any misunderstandings or communication errors that may be causing the disagreement.

Once you have a better understanding of the problem's root causes, you can begin to solve it. To accommodate your child's needs, you can consider making a nocturnal concession or coming up with a strategy to make bedtime more flexible. You may also acknowledge any mistakes you may have made, such as failing to communicate the bedtime or failing to consistently enforce it. By taking these steps, you can attempt to resolve the issue and restore trust and understanding with your child.

Parenting involves inevitable and frequent conflicts with your child. You can find solutions that work for everyone and enhance your relationship with your child if you take the time to identify and address the root causes of these conflicts. You can effectively resolve conflicts and improve communication with your child by asking open-ended questions, recognizing your own role in the conflict, and searching for ways to make concessions.

Chapter 15: Setting Boundaries And Establishing Rules

Parenting involves many different aspects, like creating norms and limits. They provide kids with a feeling of stability and order and help them grasp what is expected of them. Boundaries and regulations also assist parents in establishing boundaries and directing their children's conduct, which may foster happier and more wholesome relationships within the family.

When raising a kid, there are many different approaches to creating limits and guidelines. Being specific and consistent with your expectations is one strategy. This entails stating explicitly what actions are permitted and prohibited as well as constantly upholding the established norms. For instance, it's crucial to regularly enforce whatever rules you have about your child's arrival home from school on school evenings and to avoid making any exceptions. This demonstrates to your kid that you take your words seriously and that you expect them to abide by the rules.

Being fair and tough also helps to create limits and regulations. This entails establishing boundaries that are fair and suitable for your child's age and stage of development, and continuously upholding those boundaries. For instance, even if your kid begs or asks you to make an exception, it is crucial to continuously enforce your rules and not give in to exception-seeking behavior. Your kid will learn from this that you are in charge and that they must abide by your rules.

When enforcing limits and regulations, it's also crucial to be consistent with your punishments. This entails enforcing the penalties you previously established for certain behavior. It's crucial to constantly carry out the consequence of not letting your kid watch television if, for instance, you have a rule that they must do their schoolwork before viewing television. This helps to stress the value of obeying the rules and teaches your youngster that there are repercussions for breaking them.

When it comes to screen time, setting limits and adopting guidelines might be beneficial. Many parents find it difficult to restrict how much time their kid spends using screens, whether it be for television, computer use, or video games. To make sure that your kid is not spending too much time on screens and to encourage them to participate in other activities like reading, playing outdoors, or spending time with family and friends, it is necessary to put limitations on screen usage. You may set limitations on how much time your kid can spend using screens each day, designate periods when screens are prohibited, or impose restrictions on the kinds of material they are permitted to watch or play to create boundaries and rules surrounding screen time.

Regarding home duties and obligations, creating limits and establishing norms might be beneficial in another situation. Getting kids to pitch in around the home and accept responsibility for their actions is a challenge for many parents. You might assign certain tasks to each kid, define completion dates for tasks, and establish penalties for not finishing tasks to build limits and regulations around home duties. You might forbid your kid from watching television until their room is tidy, for instance, if they repeatedly fail to clean their room. This teaches your kid that they are accountable for their actions and that breaking the law has repercussions.

In conclusion, creating limits and standards are crucial aspects of parenting that may contribute to a feeling of peace, security, and structure within the family. You may successfully set boundaries and standards that will help direct your kid's conduct and foster a pleasant and respectful connection between you and your child by being clear and consistent with your expectations, firm and fair with your limitations, and consistent with your punishments.

Chapter 16: Expressly And Seriously

This is not a book written by Larry King to help you better your vocabulary or language skills. However, because words have such a significant impact on communication, you must pay close attention to how you use and select them.

The phrase "THE FASHION" is a word.

According to author Mark Twain, the distinction between the approximate term and the real word is a significant one. It is comparable to how the illumination of a firefly and a lightning strike appear distinct. Remember that the correct word is truly a simple one. And language is always straightforward to comprehend.

The rapid spread of new terms has resulted from the modern society's tremendous growth in knowledge. Be cautious, however, as many new terms that appear to be "in" will fail to evoke emotion in your audience.

For example, I believe you should specify "office," "home," "electricity-water pipe," and "highway" rather than relying on the phrases "mechanical" infrastructure, "macro," and "micro" exclusively.

"Don't use jargon," advised the proprietor of a radio station to his employees. Use" ("Do not use the word use. Please use that phrase!"). Clearly, "utilize" is employed less frequently than "use."

Instead of using standard, well-known terminology, many individuals prefer to employ trendy terms. Some even use slang expressions to say "that's what's trendy and new." It would be regrettable if you adopted a "trendy" mode of communication at the expense of a straightforward and comfortable one. If people understand you better, you will progress more rapidly. Additionally, you should avoid vernacular phrases that intrigue you but are not commonly used. The primary objective of communication is for the recipient to comprehend you. Therefore, they must first speak your vernacular.

TEACHING REQUIREMENTS

You should avoid using phrases such as "paradise on earth," which may sound appealing but do not help people appreciate themselves. Because sentences with excessively irregular language make it challenging to comprehend your message. Then, to ensure their comprehension, you must describe in great detail. Or, individuals may repeatedly furrow their brows when speaking.

Use caution when employing a new or contemporary expression. Do not make the other individual feel uneasy or uncomfortable. These are advantages that cannot be attained by communicating in a normal, everyday manner.

Unimportant Words

Words that are not part of our vocabulary but that confuse what we are attempting to communicate and cause others to hear unimportant information can be quite detrimental at times. A listening session. Then why do we speak these words? They resemble crutches, which are required to prevent hobbling.

Numerous English speakers have a propensity for repeatedly stating "you know." My Washington, D.C. friend always begins his statements with the phrase "You know what?" A different acquaintance, aware of this practice, made an effort to count the number of times he used the phrase in a 20-minute meeting. According to statistics, "You know what" appears 91 times! That means the man in Washington will utter "you know" approximately four and a half times per minute. I am uncertain as to whether the 91-word phrase "you know" or the discussion's topics are more enduring. If you take the story paradigm seriously, despite its absurdity, the problem is concerning. Could the "you know" man communicate effectively if he allowed the habit to take over? A minor propensity that could cause minor harm. Not to mention how extremely dull the audience is. However, do you frequently commence your sentences with "you know"?

Similar to this, use caution when beginning sentences with phrases such as "essentially," "usually," "anyway," and "hopefully" ... Try paying close attention the next time you are watching the evening news to see if the announcer repeats these phrases. Notify "Guinness World Records" if you observe that each sentence contains only one word.

In fact, I concur that it is sometimes necessary to emphasize a point using these expressions. Although your intention is to simply announce that the party will be held tomorrow night, it is not a good idea to go overboard with phrases such as "I hope to throw a party tomorrow night." Consequently, is the word "hopefully" necessary? Moreover, individuals will interpret your message differently.

Try to avoid overusing words in your sentences, regardless of the subject matter. These words can be harmful when they "sneak" into a discourse. Close your mouth and say exactly what you mean.

USE EXACT LANGUAGE

Given the wide variety of modern uses of the word, this issue is not readily resolved. I am ashamed to bring up this topic. However, we also make an effort to investigate and evaluate it, whether we like it or not.

The precise selection of words can reveal something about the status of the speaker or their attitude toward society in general. There are outmoded values and judgments in a swiftly changing society. As an illustration, I use the fact that women now play a larger role in society. So, is it acceptable to call them "weak sex"? Back then, black people were frequently described with ethnic slurs. Numerous professions are currently dominated by people of color, particularly in athletics. Similarly, the importance of the right to equality without discrimination is increasing. Historically referred to as "black slaves," it is now necessary to use the term "African American." Currently, the correct term is "Asian," whereas in the past it was "yellow-skinned oriental people" (Asian). Previously known as "Hispanic," Latino is now known as "Latino." Any ethnic community desires to be addressed with regard by their origin name. The Washington Post once published a catalog of the names of immigrants who entered the country over time in order to demonstrate progress. In 1987, the term "African-American" appeared 42 times in a single publication; by 1993, its occurrence had increased to 1,422 times.

This information demonstrates how far we have progressed in the intellectual conflict. Words have evolved to express greater reverence for numerous peoples. Carelessness with the appropriate language will place you at a significant disadvantage.

Exists a distinction between skepticism and trust? Is there a reason for our reluctance to replace "female" with "lady"? Obviously, not every woman qualifies as a lady. Nevertheless, the word has been recognized. You have the choice of using or not using. This issue was presented by a female editor of a small magazine and another male editor.

You may be a bit hasty when you tell a female colleague in the workplace, "You look amazing in this blouse!" or "This outfit makes you so attractive!" It is currently advised to exercise caution when extending praise. The highest compliment is "This dress is gorgeous!"

However, does it not also appear moderate and "remaining"? However, it is safe. Safety is currently the most essential factor. "What is there is what is there" occurs in the film "The King and I" (The King and I). No is not what is. Now, however, everything is in pandemonium. Throughout the film, the king's comments are comical but not completely absurd. What transpired? Things that were once stigmatized are now tolerated. Some behaviors that were acceptable in the past are now unacceptable. In addition, the contemporary word sea is disorganized. Therefore, using inappropriate language can be detrimental.

Eliminate your awful speech-reading behaviors.

How do you implement subpar behavior? Remember these three strategies:

Simply stated, pay attention to the first words that come out of your mouth. You must monitor your own speech while speaking. You must be aware of when to stop and when to proceed. How frequently have you paused before saying "Well, uh"? These are the worms that produce your communication.

Second, arrange what you will say prior to speaking. I am aware of how challenging this is. We occasionally fail to complete a phrase, which causes us anxiety. I do not imply that you must compose an entire speech before stepping up to the microphone. Nevertheless, you can formulate the second statement while delivering the first. If you find this task too difficult, try practicing more. Then, you'll realize that it's entirely possible, and you'll shortly have to master it. You can certainly conjure up two issues simultaneously. If we understand how to use our brain, it can be extraordinarily beneficial.

Third, construct a "check board" to monitor your speech and quickly correct any errors. The "Inspection Board" will immediately communicate "Stop or Zap" - (Stop or Continue!) to you. Who is the "inspection board"? Are any of your friends situated in the section beneath you? By their glimpses and subtle hand movements, you can determine the nature of the situation. This has an unanticipated outcome. Friends' support means that you are not speaking alone and can do so with assurance. I guarantee that you will acquire a flawless command of the English language with consistent practice.

Chapter 17: Resolve The Underlying Tensions In Your Relationships.

In order to resolve the tension in our relationships, we have determined that a Relationship Reset, or a fresh start, is necessary. You may be wondering at this point, "Why is resetting a relationship so important?" That is a fair issue. In fact, it is perfectly reasonable to question whether a Relationship Reset is even a "thing." Considering that we are all in relationships with friends and family, why can't we just let things be? Even if there are forbidden subjects in the relationship, you may have normalized not discussing them, so why "rock the boat"? In some relationships, you may have acted as if "the event" had never occurred. At the very least, you may feel that you are superficially conversing with each other, which is an improvement over the past. In addition, you may believe there is nothing you can or should do to better your interactions with one another.

Well, here's the truth: Even if you know there are topics you no longer discuss with someone and you believe you've moved on, the likelihood is that you have not, in fact, moved on. Or perhaps one individual has moved past it while another has not. It is also possible that one or both of you are in various stages of attempting to resolve the situation. And this is why, my peers, you should strive to share the same understanding of the relationship. Essentially, the relationship you have now will continue into the future. If you do not make a concerted effort to work on yourself and the relationship, your strained relationship will be subject to whatever and whoever comes along, without any guiding principles.

Tension's Symptoms Serve as Our Compass

When you hear the term "guideposts," rules may come to mind. This is not exactly what I have in mind. For our purposes, "guideposts" are the relationship symptoms triggered by specific events. We learned in Chapter 2 why we must cultivate a communication perspective in order to initiate a Relationship Reset. Additionally, we discovered that there are symptoms associated with the tension in our relationships. As we have previously discussed, situations that directly affect us have a ripple effect on our relationships with others. Frequently, we are unaware of what is occurring, and if we are, we may choose to disregard it. We may experience the emotion caused by it, but we do not address it. We let go of our emotions because we do not want to make a huge deal out of something or cause an argument. Or we attempt to explain it away as if it were not what we believe it to be.

These sentiments and emotions serve as our compass. These markers provide us with direction. They informed us that there is a way forward. While the path ahead may be unknown, we are pointed in the right direction. The symptoms that we experience as a result of the tension lead us in the same direction.

Guideposts are advantageous because they inform us what we need to communicate in the moment. Guideposts are predicated on what is occurring within us that is unseen by others. They are our feelings, emotions, experiences, and perspectives that we would not ordinarily share; however, they alert us to the possibility of connecting with a close relationship partner. Guideposts are sentiments such as, "Oh my gosh, you're still doing this after all these years?" Or, "I should be honest about what actually transpired." This is contrary to the social advice you may have heard: "If you have nothing nice to say, don't say anything at all." The distinction lies in the type of relationship as well as the relational objectives. When referring to a Relationship Reset, we mean working on a relationship with a past and the exchange of personal experiences. For a reset to occur and for the guideposts to be meaningful, the relationship must be meaningful. Moreover, the purpose of the relationship should be to resolve the tension, improve the relationship, and foster intimacy. This is a relationship we wish to strengthen.

Which personal relationship would you choose as the one in which you encounter tension-related symptoms? The majority of us are aware of precisely which relationship and how long the tension has existed. Consider the last time you considered not bringing up the taboo subject. Were you conversing with a pal? Your dad? Your cousin? How did you feel after the interaction in which you did not express your emotions? I suspect that it is not very excellent. Moreover, guess what? Typically, these unresolved emotions surface repeatedly, when you least expect them, and have an effect not only on you but also on the relationship.

When communication fails, the issue does not vanish. In fact, it festers and causes even worse symptoms. As the years pass and the passage of time drags on, so does the tension. Contrary to the ancient adage, time alone does not heal anything.

So, what is the remedy? How do we use our compass points to progress toward the Relationship Reset? First, you must determine the cause of the symptoms. Ask yourself, "Where is the tension really coming from?" Is the tension a result of the relationship's context? Or have you allowed other experiences to infect this relationship? Exists tension in the current moment? Or is it from somewhere along the continuum of communication? Remember that we discussed how communication flows along a timeline, and it is entirely conceivable for this person to have unresolved tension from months or years ago.

Everything we are learning is based on communication, but there is also an element of psychology, as this process requires us to be honest with ourselves about the hidden truths in our minds. Even though I am not a psychologist, therapist, counselor, or psychiatrist, I believe there is value in spending time "on the couch." Mental health is equivalent to physical wellbeing. All aspects of your health are important: emotional, spiritual, mental, physical, financial, and relational well-being. Dealing with the tension in your relationships or within your family may require the assistance of a professional who can help you identify the source of the tension and comprehend how it impacts your life.

The tension may be caused by an internal or external influence. What is the distinction? Well, internal influence indicates that whatever is causing the tension occurred over the course of the relationship and involved the parties involved. External influence implies that the tension is caused by something or someone unrelated to the relationship, but that the tension is contaminating the relationship.

Let's place this into context and revisit our earlier conversation about the matter. You may be avoiding the friend because when you both got married years ago, you made a vow that you would never cheat on your spouses, and now it feels like a lie. That is an internal factor. Or, you may be avoiding the friend because you once had an affair, and your friend's behavior reminds you of your own transgressions. That too is internal. Consider internal to be something that you do or say to yourself. Your internal dialogue can generate tension. Now, if the friend dictates that you keep certain secrets regarding the affair from other friends or family members, this is external. Someone or something is acting upon you. What do you do when these kinds of problems arise? Do you acquiesce because it seems easier? However, the issue is: simpler than what? And more convenient for whom? You probably have no idea what the alternative would be. You may believe that you are aware of what will be said and how the situation will develop. However, you truly do not. More doubts exist than answers.

These are the difficult concerns we must all constantly address. Even more importantly, you are likely asking yourself these queries. This has everything to do with you and nothing to do with the other person. Important is the origin of why you feel the way you do about the topic. This comprehension is required to initiate the restore procedure. If you intend to begin something new, you must be willing to dismantle the old system.

The majority of the time, the old system we operate from is based on how we interpret and function in the world around us, and those in our inner circle learn to adapt to it. Why do they act this way? Since they adore us. They believe they are demonstrating affection by avoiding upsetting us and not creating problems where none exist. Therefore, we employ alternatives, adjustments, and modifications to maintain the system. We become more committed to the system than to the friendship at some point.

Due to our long-term relationships, we respond based on the knowledge we possess. Let's return to the example of the occurrence and observe the situation as an outsider. It is likely that both individuals have cheated on their spouses in the past and have developed a system within their friendship to accommodate infidelity. They have determined signals and developed a code for use. For instance, if one receives a phone call from the other, they know to ask, "What time are we meeting up for drinks?" This is code for "my spouse is listening in." I'm saying this out loud so that you are aware that I'm leaving for the evening. If you receive a phone call or text message searching for me, you know where I am and with whom I am." You may find this bizarre, but this is how many individuals "do" relationships.

In order for a system to exist, regardless of the system's nature, the system must be supported by individuals and institutions. There must be mutual understanding through communication. This is the only way the system can function. Relationships function similarly. We fight to maintain the system regardless of whether it's dysfunctional, unhealthy, toxic, or hazardous, so relationships exist in whatever state they're in. In light of this fact, the only way for a relationship to function differently is to recalibrate the system.

The Refresh

I must be honest and confess that initiating a Relationship Reset can be messy because we are disrupting the relationship's status quo. You are causing systemic disruption. Whether they acknowledge it or not, most individuals in relationships play a role. Frequently, we did not choose the role; it was thrust upon us by the relationship's context and circumstances. You may be the "mother" who always gives advice and direction, for instance. You may be the "caretaker" who ensures that the individual consumes their medications and remains sober. You may be the "protector" who is always present at family functions in order to shield an acquaintance from their mother's toxic relationship. This is by no means an exhaustive list, as we can perform numerous roles within our families and relationships. However, when the roles alter abruptly, resistance occurs.

Establishing a new normal for the relationship may appear to be a daunting and, quite candidly, impossible task. You are establishing new norms and boundaries, which could result in a shift in roles. Some roles could even be eliminated entirely. To some, stating that people have roles in a relationship implies that we are to some degree acting. That is just. Consider however: Since acting is not real, there may be aspects of the relationship that are not real. Resetting is a method to stop acting. It enables us to function as our genuine selves in the relationship, thereby enhancing what is already present.

When you engage in a Relationship Reset, you acknowledge that the way the relationship previously functioned or the role you previously played no longer applies. Although it may seem counterintuitive to place on your oxygen mask, you must do so Prior to assisting others, it is not admirable for two individuals to perish needlessly. In the context of a relationship, it makes no sense for those involved to carry the emotional baggage associated with forbidden subjects that are infecting the relationship.

Before genuine change can occur, the relationship must be dismantled. This concept may appear destructive. That is precisely the case. You are dismantling your preconceived conceptions regarding how you feel about past events. You are demolishing the wall of secrecy and stigma surrounding the forbidden subject. But you are not doing the following: You are not initiating a debate. This is neither an attack nor a trap. Remember that you are cultivating a communication mindset. You approach the individual and the prohibited subject differently. Why? Because what you have been doing has not been effective. This is not about assigning fault. It is not your responsibility that your previous strategies have failed. Remember that you passively learned communication skills from external forces.

In the next chapter, we will examine the primary reasons why so many of us continue to struggle in this area of relationships. We will discuss communication barriers that prevent us from being the most effective communicators possible. Then, following the relational dismantling, we will sift through the debris to determine what salvageable elements are viable. Finding the courage to continue forward will also be required for this process. As you might expect, this portion of the procedure will require considerable effort from both parties, but it is possible. You will emerge from this situation in a stronger position than you are currently in. You will be more powerful because you will be equipped with tools that enable you to focus on the strength of the relationship and the other individual. These qualities will keep you rooted in your commitment to the relationship and to one another, as opposed to your commitment to the system.

We will conclude by discussing relationship terminations. Inconvenient as it may be, sometimes it makes the most sense for individuals to no longer communicate with one another. Certainly, ceasing all communication may not be a mutual decision, but it is one that should be considered and honored if made.

While it may appear that you are focusing on the other individual, you are actually concentrating on yourself. You owe it to yourself and the other person to right any past wrongs, acknowledge your genuine experiences, and choose to have a new relationship that moves in a better direction moving forward.

Conclusion

Public speaking entails delivering a speech or presentation in front of an audience. It is essential in a variety of professional and personal contexts because it enables individuals to convey information, persuade others, and entertain an audience.

Numerous factors, including stage anxiety, preparation and practice, mindfulness and relaxation techniques, and the use of effective body language and eye contact, can affect public speaking performance. Obtaining assistance from friends, family, or a public speaking coach can also aid in overcoming stage anxiety and enhancing public speaking performance.

Confidence is an essential element of effective public speaking. Confidence can help individuals engage an audience, effectively communicate their message, and manage challenging questions and situations. Developing self-acceptance and confidence through experience can assist individuals in delivering successful public speeches.

Individuals can enhance their public speaking skills and deliver effective speeches by understanding and addressing these factors.

www.ingramcontent.com/pod-product-compliance
Lightning Source LLC
Chambersburg PA
CBHW050233120526
44590CB00016B/2063